Charles T. Griffes

I0803685

POEM

for Flute and Piano

Edited by

JAMES GALWAY

Piano Reduction by Phillip Moll

GREAT PERFORMER'S EDITION

ED-3870

ISBN 978-0-7935-5626-7

G. SCHIRMER, *Inc.*

DISTRIBUTED BY

HAL•LEONARD® CORPORATION

7777 W. BLUEMOUND RD. P.O. BOX 13819 MILWAUKEE, WI 53213

Introductory Note

Charles T. Griffes' *Poem* for flute and orchestra was first performed on November 16, 1919 by the New York Symphony Orchestra with its principal flutist, Georges Barrère, as soloist and Walter Damrosch conducting. It was a great success, but its unfortunate composer died less than half a year later at the age of 35. The last contract Griffes signed with G. Schirmer was for the publication of the *Poem.* The orchestral score, however, did not appear in print until 1951. In 1922 Schirmer published an arrangement by Barrère for flute and piano. Barrère was a good friend and frequent collaborator of Griffes and was well acquainted with the composer's intentions. On the other hand, he was not a pianist and it is our feeling that his reduction omits too much orchestral material, which not only adds interest and color, but also helps the flutist who is preparing for a performance with orchestra to form a clearer idea of what to listen for in the accompaniment. Our wish has been to restore as much as possible without having the piano part sound cluttered or making it awkward to play.

About the Text

The musical text of this edition is based on the flute and piano version of 1922 and on the 1951 study score, both published by G. Schirmer. There are some discrepancies between these editions and the very clear autograph manuscript, which is in the New York Public Library at Lincoln Center. Most of these discrepancies are slight and some changes are probably attributable to Barrère. For example, the rhythm and articulation in the flute part in mm. 211–212, 215–216, 227–228, and 231–232 is, 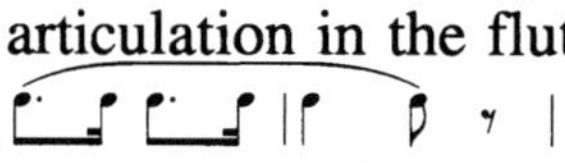 in the autograph score . Barrère no doubt concluded that the articulation,  along with the double-dotted rhythm, yielded a crisper result. Similarly, at mm. 209, 213, 225, and 229, the manuscript shows no staccato dots.

Three pitch variants deserve mention. In m. 147, the printed editions have F sharp as the next to last sixteenth note in the flute part. This is evidently a misreading. Also in the flute part in m. 181, the second sixteenth note is A sharp in the printed editions. However, in view of the sharp before the A on the eighth sixteenth note and the natural before the last sixteenth of that bar, both of which are quite clear in the autograph, it seems irrefutable that Griffes did indeed intend for A natural to be played here. Finally, in m. 113, although there is no disagreement between the manuscript and the printed versions, Samuel Baron, who studied the *Poem* with Barrère, reports that Barrère told him the first sixteenth note should be B flat and that he performed it that way himself. There is no question that Griffes wrote a natural here.

In the final analysis, performers, using the best available information, must rely on their own judgement and taste to resolve these questions. A more detailed discussion of the *Poem* can be found in Donna K. Anderson's excellent article "The Griffes Poem: A New Perspective," published in the Newsletter of the National Flute Association, Volume VIII, No. 1, Fall 1982.

—Phillip Moll

POEM

Charles T. Griffes
Edited by James Galway
Piano reduction by Phillip Moll

16
20
B Poco più mosso
dim.
mf
p
24
pp
28
rit.
C Tranquillamente
f
dim. molto
pp

32
poco cresc.
cresc.
Ped.
36
42
accel.
cresc.
45
poco rit.
a tempo
dim.
espr.

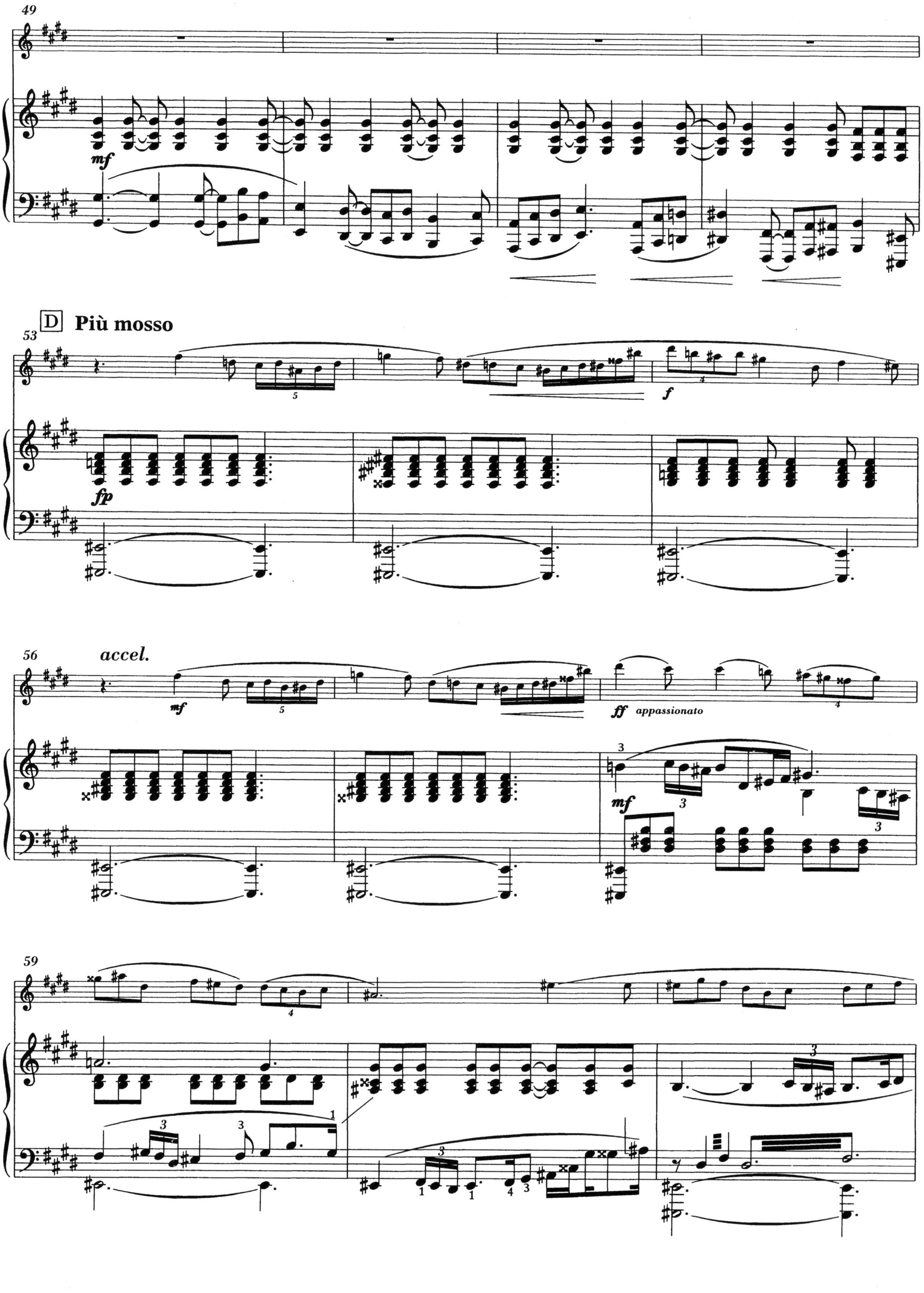
49
53
D
Più mosso
56
accel.
appassionato
59

E Più mosso
62
cresc.
cresc.
ff
f
65
mf
68
agitato
p
cresc.
f
f
p
71
poco rit.
mf
p
mf
cresc.
f

F
75
tranquillo
p
pp
80
p
pp
rit.
p espr.
84
Tempo I
Poco più mosso
f
p espr.
90
G
pp
f

Charles T. Griffes

POEM

for Flute and Piano

Edited by

JAMES GALWAY

Piano Reduction by Phillip Moll

Flute

GREAT PERFORMER'S EDITION

ED-3870
ISBN 978-0-7935-5626-7

G. SCHIRMER, *Inc.*

DISTRIBUTED BY
HAL•LEONARD® CORPORATION
7777 W. BLUEMOUND RD. P.O. BOX 13819 MILWAUKEE, WI 53213

Flute

POEM

Charles T. Griffes
edited by James Galway

49
D Più mosso
4
f
56
accel.
mf
ff appassionato
59
cresc.
E Più mosso
63
ff
67
70
f agitato
73
poco rit.
F tranquillo
mf
p
p
78
pp
p
82
rit.
Tempo I
Poco più mosso
3
3
pp
91
G

96
pp
p
101
p agitato
105
accel.
cresc.
108
(cresc.)
110
f
7
113
rit.
mf
dim.
H Allegro scherzando
116
p
122
128
I
f
134
p

J
K
Poco meno mosso
Più mosso

L Con fuoco
cresc.
dim.
M Vivace
N poco a poco accel.
Presto

ff
dim.
sempre dim.
O Tempo I
pp
pp
poco rit.
P
a tempo
pp
p
dim.
pp

95
pp
p
dim.
pp trem.
100
agitato
p
f
dim.
p
104
accel.
cresc.
cresc.
108
(cresc.)

112
rit.
dim.
116
H Allegro scherzando
122
sempre pp
128
I

134
p
pp
139
f
p
144
p
pp
f
148
J
p

152
156
1
161
p
166
f
sf
f

K Poco meno mosso
171
Ped.
176
181
Più mosso
p cantabile
con pedale
184

188
p
cresc.
p
cresc.
193
L Con fuoco
f
f
mf
197
f
201

205
dim.
dim.
209
M Vivace
f
mf
sim.
senza pedale
214
mf
219
cresc.

N poco a poco accel.
224
f
f
4
229
mf
mp
234
cresc.
mf
239
Presto
cresc.
ff
f

245
mf
sf
250
dim.
sempre dim.
259
O
Tempo I
pp
p
pp
264
poco rit.
a tempo
pp
mf

P
268
espr.
272
277
dim.
282